WHY WE PLEDGE ALLEGIANCE

By Dillon Krueger

Dedicated to my boys
Liam, Maddox, and Asher Krueger

Try to find all 31 feathers!

Copyright 2025 by Real Patriot Publishing, LLC
All rights reserved.

WHY WE PLEDGE ALLEGIANCE

Today is a very exciting day for the young American bald eagle named Georgie...

But as he RUNS down his road he remembers something...

THAT'S WHERE THE BEAST LIVES!

HE IS FROZEN WITH FEAR!

He opens his eyes and realizes, "that's no beast. it's just Dawson the bison pulling the school wagon."

"Good morning, Georgie," Dawson says.
"I hope you're ready for your first day of school.

Lets go pick up your friends!"

Georgie is the first kid to be picked up! The wagon makes multiple stops. They pick up...

Asher the armadillo,

Liam the mountain lion,

Maddox the moose,

Allie the alligator,

and Tanner the turkey!

Once all the students have been picked up, Dawson the bison pulls the school wagon up a long winding trail...

...UNTIL FINALLY THEY ARRIVE AT THE SCHOOL!

All the students are greeted by an American bald eagle. It's Georgie's mom! "Good morning class," she says. "I'm your new teacher, Mrs. Washington."

"We have a lot of great things to learn today but first we need to do something very important. We need to recite The Pledge of Allegiance."

"Now everyone please stand up, face the flag, and put your right hand...

OR WING,

OR PAW,

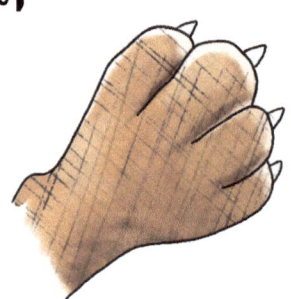

OR CLAW,

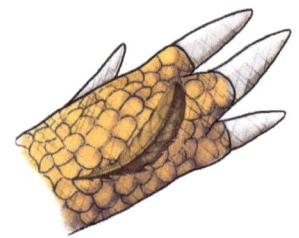

OR HOOF,

OR WEBBED FOOT

OVER YOUR HEART, AND REPEAT AFTER ME."

"I pledge allegiance to the flag of the United States of America, and to the republic for which it stands, one nation, under God, indivisible, with liberty and justice for all."

"Now let's learn about the parts of the flag," she continues.

"The color WHITE represents Purity and Innocence.

This reminds us that our country must remain a place where people can live free."

"The American flag has 50 stars on a blue field, also called the canton. They represent all 50 states.

The color BLUE symbolizes Vigilance, Perseverance, and Justice.

This means we should always stay watchful and strong."

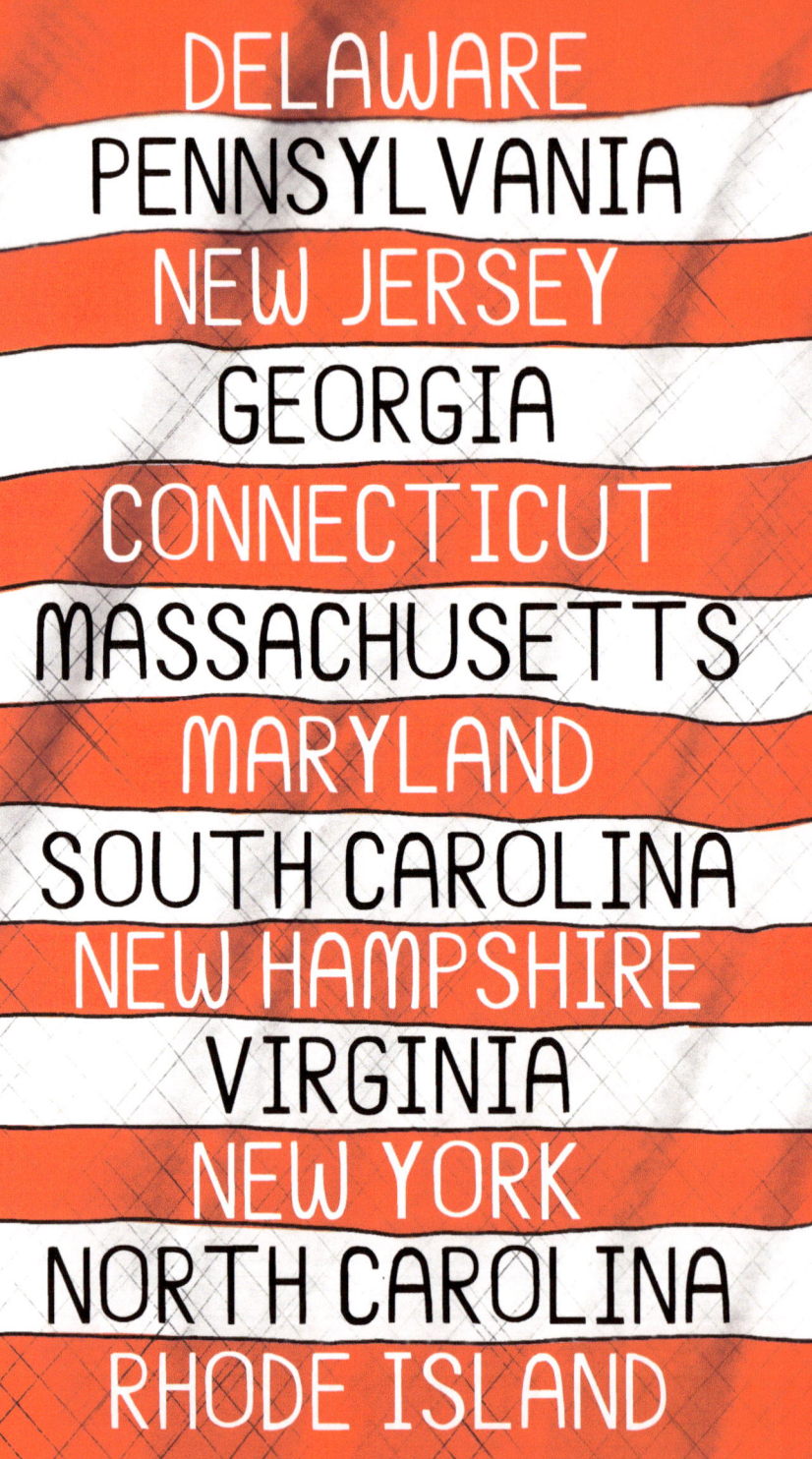

"The flag has 13 stripes, 7 red and 6 white. These represent the 13 British Colonies that declared independence from Great Britain and became the first states!

The color RED symbolizes Valor and Bravery.

This is to remember the blood shed by those who have fought to protect our country."

Liam the mountain lion raises his paw and asks, "Why do we pledge allegiance to the flag?"

"That's a great question." Mrs. Washington responds.

"The Pledge is a promise to be true to the United States of America. It was created in 1892 by Francis Bellamy to teach children patriotism by having them recite it every day before school. To be a patriot means you love your country and don't take our freedom for granted. We are proud to be Americans."

"Every part of this oath has a special meaning."

"WE PLEDGE ALLEGIANCE...
We promise to be true to the United States of America

TO THE FLAG...
The American flag is our nation's symbol

OF THE UNITED STATES OF AMERICA...
Our country, made up of 50 states

AND TO THE REPUBLIC...
A republic is a country where the people choose their representatives to make laws for them

FOR WHICH IT STANDS...
The flag, meaning the country

ONE NATION...
A single nation

UNDER GOD...
The people believe in a supreme being

INDIVISIBLE...
The country cannot be split

WITH LIBERTY AND JUSTICE FOR ALL."
With freedom and fairness for every American citizen

"We Pledge Allegiance to the flag because the American flag is very special and should always be treated with HONOR and RESPECT.

The STARS and STRIPES bring us together as citizens by reminding us of the sacrifices made for our FREEDOM and the values AMERICA stands for...

LIFE, LIBERTY, and the PURSUIT of HAPPINESS."

At the end of the day all of the kids are excited to go home and share what they have learned.

Georgie has conquered his fear of the beast at the end of the road and looks forward to going to school tomorrow to recite the Pledge of Allegiance again, but first...

...HE NEEDS TO COLOR HIS NEW FAVORITE PICTURE.

Follow Real Patriot Publishing for more great patriotic content!

INSTAGRAM

FACEBOOK

YOUTUBE

About The Author:

Dillon Krueger served in the United States Army Infantry and was deployed to Afghanistan during Operation Enduring Freedom in 2011. "Why We Pledge Allegiance" was created to teach children what the American flag represents as well as the values of patriotism. Dillon believes as American citizens we owe it to those brave men and women who have made the ultimate sacrifice for this nation, and the Gold Star families, to say the Pledge of Allegiance in schools every morning.

It is Dillon's hope that other parents can find value in "Why We Pledge Allegiance" and our society will continue to raise our children to be proud American citizens.

Real Patriot Publishing was started to deliver the message of patriotism among children. Look for the first book in Dillon's Young Patriots series "Why We Stand!"

www.ingramcontent.com/pod-product-compliance
Lightning Source LLC
Chambersburg PA
CBHW051513110526
44582CB00008B/152